LIFE PART 2

WHITE LAVENDER

I dedicate my work to life and my loved ones.

Life teaches us about everything and nothing, it gives us the means to be.

Our loved ones teach us about everything and nothing too, they make our life full of emotions, they give us reasons to feel and experience those different emotions, they are with us all the time in our hearts and share their love for us in their own ways, be it small or big.

I dedicate this book to all of them who have given me the reason to exist, and to those too who gave me the means to exist.

Contents

Contents

1. Natures Night

With the wind moving
And the birds grooving
I live like a jellyfish
As I wish
For an end to come
As I hum
The song of my past
Carrying hope vast
Swimming in the water shallow
Breathing in air callow
Sat there
Under the nature's care
Mesmerized by the sight
Of the night.

2. Why The Discrimination

When you meet someone new

As a child

You don't ask for their view

As they are very mild

Passed from their parents to them

As the time passed by

They are just another gem

Waiting to be tossed in the sky

They are just another friend

For you to spend time with

Following all the new trend

And chat about the myth

You don't judge them on their caste

Or their religion

You just have some blast

Without discrimination even a smidgen

Why can't one follow that all their life

And be happy
While not having any strife
Or being snappy
The world is not at all
But atleast we can try
Like trying not to start a brawl
And not making innocents cry.

3. Time To Change

With every step you took

You made everyone look

At you and your goal

Playing leaders role

With every rule you create

A new future you illustrate

Gave them hope

Who needed it to cope

From the deeply poisoned world

With words as if twistedly curled

No knowledge of what to be done

With people who killed for fun

Other than to end them

And start cutting the stem

Of the widespread criminal net

Who kill with their pet

Roaming around free

Going on shopping spree

Thinking they are above everyone

And taking away people's bread as well as bun
It's time for them to stop
And us to not eat their crop
It's time to change
And narrow down their working range
Which nothing else to do
It will forcefully stop them as well as their crew

4. Changes In Life

<u>***You have been warned:*** *The following situation in the poem is 100% imagination and is not aimed at anyone. Any similarities found are totally coincidental.*</u>

I sat for two years waiting for you
And you didn't have a single clue
Every time you called me your brother
My mind gave a shudder
I wanted you as a lover
But my so-called best friend had taken that cover
I sat there watching everything
As to him you were just another fling
When he broke your heart
I knew it was the time to dart
Not across the ocean blue
But towards you
I took my chance
While drinking some wine in France
Under the beautiful starry night
Which were shining very bright
While you were looking fantastically
Sitting there smiling enthusiastically
The sight printed in my heart deep

Even today while we sleep
After 30 years of our marriage
In which you stepped down the carriage
After you agreed to marry me
And make our own family tree.

5. Tale Of My Life

You have been warned: _The following situation in the poem is 100% imagination and is not aimed at anyone. Any similarities found are totally coincidental._

When you adopted me

I was barely four

I thought it was my freedom's key

All the while thinking that you loved me from your very hearts

core

I did everything to please you

All the while I grew

Then all I know was the baby arrived

As I saw towards the hospital you drived

I loved the baby with all my heart

Even when I overheard something that made me dart

Towards my room

While millions of thoughts began to loom

As I laid there

When nobody truly cared

On my bed

My head filled with dread

I knew it

That I would never fit

No matter how much I tried

No matter how much cried

You never truly gave me your love

It was all truly a glove

You truly never cared

As its the baby you bared

Not me

I wonder if I am even on the family tree

At least dad cared

As it was him who dared

To look over me

After I flee

One day came what I feared

It started with you acting weird

We went on a drive

Then you left me to strive

All alone in the orphanage

Without any words as if you didn't have any courage

I took a deep breath

And started walking hoping it won't lead to my death

All by myself

Wishing that I could be an elf

So with just one click

I would reach home with a single flick

Won't have to walk in the rain

With my feet throbbing in pain

And when I reached back home

You simply handed me a comb
And then made an excuse
Flat out ignoring my bruise
I knew you didn't love me
But to hate me to this degree
I acted as if I believed you
Then retired to my room after removing my shoe
Dad saw this all
Standing near the wall
But said nothing out loud
And you were secretly on the cloud
As your plan started then and there
And you stopped showing any care
It was the day
Despite my numerous pray
You stopped being my mother
All was left were my dad and my brother
At least they loved me
Even if we couldn't go on a shopping spree
I grew up with their love and your hate
But we all have our own fate.
Today we are in our own places
Running our own races in our life
We are both happy with what have in our life
It's still a wonder how we lived together with so much strife.
And I do believe
That it's how we should continue to live.

6. My Life My Choice

My life's goal won't be belied

Finally, it is my happiness that has taken a glide

While thinking back on the memories I packed

It's truly family's love that I lacked

My life ain't a game

Which you can burn into the flame

It's mine and mine alone

Just like the throne

I decide what to do with it

Be myself or try to fit

Where I don't belong

Even after knowing it's very wrong

No thanks

It's my turn to climb the ranks

To where I belong

Announcing the truth with a gong

For it's my turn

To have some fun

Yours is to burn

As it's what you will truly earn

If ever in the future do something

While I relax in the hot spring

I have earned it
And all that without ever throwing a fit

7. Uncertain Future Of Our Love

Last time I met you

You didn't have any clue

Of who I am

With our faces covered with jam

Blue and red

On our faces instead of bread

We had so much fun

Even if we couldn't have any fruit bun

For all we knew

We were part of the crew

Came to work

Even as a clerk

On a run

Without any gun

We were so happy

Without being sappy

I still remember your smile

When we were hiding in the asile
The sparkle in your eye
When we went for a fly
Best of the best
Even if it's just for a test
I want you to be happy forever
Even if our relationship gets over
The future ain't certain
As it's hidden behind the curtain
We'll wait and watch
As the only thing which matters is our happiness being
top-notch.

8. Life & It's Danger

What I wanted was someone to love

Someone to cherish

But what I got was someone who wanted me to hurt

And to perish

Wishes are strange

And somewhat deranged

Needs are a must

And wants turns to dust

Love ain't the work of cupid

Just as a stupid life is stupid

It's all superficial

I wonder how much of it is judicial

We deserve what we earn

And whatever we steal will always make us burn

To be fair

Its in the very air

Which we will have to clean

And make our environment green

Its to shed the fake sheen

As its always visible to the eyes as keen
As if of an eagle
Who will hunt you as if a beagle
On a prowl
With a scary growl
Looking out for us
Like an important truss
For those who live in ignorance
Life requires us to be vigorous
I can assure you it ain't fair
And no one will care
If you fail
They will simply leave you in the jail
While you will have built
With your very own guilt
Prepare for your life
It contains a lot of strife
Buck up
Hard work ain't sup
Beware of the danger
As their ain't any ranger
To rescue you out
If you caught insanities bought
All the best
For now you leave your nest
Into the real world
No time to be furled.

9. The Future Holds

I want to see
What the future holds for me
Where I go
With the time's flow
Needless to say
My life is like a clay
In my own hands to mold
The way I want it to hold
The future I want to see
And become my life's key.

10. Vow To Future

Sorting out the bindings of life
Does not happen without any strife
Life is like a butterfly wing
Which doesn't need a sling
Full of coloured dust
With no chance to gather any rust
In and out riddled with trouble
With parts of the parts rubble
There is nothing like the future I want to know
And for that, I make a vow
To do my best for everything I want
Even if it leads to changing my life's font.

11. Future's Flight

The freedom of air
Isn't present in the chair
We can do so much while flying
Like enjoying or even spying
The freedom you get there
Won't be found, even in your lair
But be cautious of what you do
As up there ain't any loo
For our future, my child
Don't consider your passion as mild
Do you want to
Make same not to wait in the queue
Not everything is black and white
And the darkness doesn't mean its night
Just as not every white dove
Represents love.

12. Truth Of The Crown

The cost of the crown

Is enough to make us frown

Death comes to everyone

And those who don't care

The throne is just a chair

The jewels are just some stones

And the burial ground is just a pit of bones

Diamonds are just tightly put together carbon

New York is just another place like Barbon

What they don't know

Is the pressure's blow

The expectations weight

Piling higher with every passing gate

The tears we shed

When in war, our people are found dead

No one truly knows

What in our mind truly goes

How we weep

When our people are killed like some harvest to reep

The enemy doesn't know our mindset

All the while internally we fret

Think over and over

While they think we are some kind of drover.

13. Plants Journey

Watching the drop of water
I recalled the plant's daughter
Very similar to its parent
Books showed me the reason apparent
Fertilized by the kind similar
Transported by the tube which was somewhat cylinder
On its complement
And a bit of a special treatment
It started to grow
The parents removed with a plow
Transported as a seed
It had a journey to lead
When reached to the destination
The bird called the station
Ejected from its ride
Reached a field wide
The soil was fertile
And river nearby was the Nile
Slowly it grew
And the leaves were taken for some kind of brew
And that's how I found it
While painting water and cat with its kit

WHITE LAVENDER

Drinking water
When the day was left only a quarter.

14. Wonder of Words

With every page I turned
New things I learned
With a large amount of glee
It gives me the energy
About the things' I write expertly
Reading stories of every kind
With a glass of wine
Learning from every line
Some with double meanings underneath
Covering a lot like a wreath
For all I know
It could be telling about a garden to mow
Which is shown as if
It's a pudding we take a sniff
It's a jumbled puzzle
Which we read while on the sofa we nuzzle.

15. My Life With You

I'll move with you

Across the ocean blue

The decision is huge

But I am ready to take refuge

Even in a town new

Going around like a wind which blew

Established a life for us

Ignoring the societies fuss

Doing what is right

Making sure not to be involved in any street fight

Earning what I own

And not snatching others' cone

Following my heart

Has been as nice as a sweet-tart

I say thank you for the food

It really was good

But I have to go

As I have a new river to row.

16. Drop of Dew, Chime of Bell

Everyone has shortcomings of their own
We shouldn't go around picking the bone
For we also have them
And it will grow more if ignored like a wild stem
Picking on others is a sign of zealotry
Broaden your approach
As it means you have to work your gauche
Everyone has their own point of view
Take the example of a drop of due
Special on its own
Even when alone
Boring after a time
Not unlike a bell's chime
Too less is not enough
No need to act tough
Too much is not needed
Even though the problem is to be weeded
You learn in your own way
Time can be the price you pay
But life ain't free

We should learn that from a bee.

17. I Wish To Be Myself

I am a person of my own
Don't judge me on the basis of the image my family has shown
I wish to be myself
Not the names of my parents given on my birth certificate which
is kept on the top shelf
I want to do something good
Which won't be judged on the basis of my mood
I wish to be known
Which will leave people's minds blown
I wish to work on my goal
Which can lighten my soul
I wish to create who I am
And be safe enough to not become a wolf's lam
I promise to work for it
Even if it leads me to be thrown into a deep pit
I will climb again with more ways
Even if it takes me more than a few days
I will do it still
Even when needed to take the artic's chill
In the end
My enemies will bend
In front of my work's result

And they will be ashamed for they gave me nothing but many
kinds of insult
I will show them all
That I can still stand up, even after taking a fall.

18. Expectations and It's Response

Expectations are huge
And imaginations become our refuge
When you told how to behave
Imagining myself as a free bird is what my mind gave
When ordered what and what not to eat
It's imagination where my mind retreat
When told what to wear
I kind of stopped even care
When told how I should have not cried
It's my brain which feels like being fried
I will do whatever my mind wants
I have stopped caring about your taunts
I will not bow down to you
Oh! Society come forward in the queue
As the same applies to you all
I won't be a puppet and answer your call
I have my own dreams
And it's you who will be backing down it seems
I have made up my mind
And its my own future I wish to find

On my own rules
Not of the fools
I wish you all the best
As I am off to my life's quest.

19. Truth Of Life & Its Cycle

What is luxury for one, is misery for other
What is happiness for one, can be the cause of sadness for other
When someone wins a bet at the same time someone loses it too
The life goes in a cycle
With no end to it
The world can end for some
And may start for other
Money is momentary
Feeling's too
But it's the memories that stay with us all through
The grains of sand are like time
Can't truly be contained as they keep flowing.
No matter how tight you hold
It will still cross the threshold
From one to other
Moving further
For those who chase it
May never truly be able to catch
As in its chase, they will miss what could have had
So open your eyes, and accept what you get

If you crave for more, then earn it
May your wishes reach to you
In whatever way possible
As we shan't chase, what truly is impossible.

20. Emotion & Life

The whirlwind of the emotion
May truly never calm
As emotions are weapons
Wielded as a norm
You can't control them
You can't leave them
If you need them as much as air
And is something which is truly can't be shared
Needless to say
It will make its way
Should tried to be stopped
We will all be chopped
The humanity will snap
Life will turn into a crap
For those who know what I mean
It's not the words destruction we learn
But that's what we will get
If we continue on this path set
Bewarn and beware
As it ain't some silly dare
It's the end we talked about
It will catch you no matter how much you shout

The decision is in your hand
And the results will show where you stand.

21. Freedom In Death or Freedom As A Path

Watching the dusk turn into dawn
I found a little fawn
Tied to a tree
Waiting to be free
Be it via death or hand
Depends on fate's stand
It knows that life would end
But it's his own life he needs to fend
Thirsty, hungry, scared
Unable to decide
Should he call for help or hide
I went ahead slowly
He watched as if its something holy
I gave him some water
He left not even a quarter
And after being freed
He ran toward his home at an amazing speed
But not without a look towards me
As if to thank me for the water even if it was from the sea
And remembering moments like those

My heart glows
For it feels that it was nthing but a dream
Which I remembered while watching a flowing stream.

22. Wish Turned Dream Turned Reality

What we wish for

Can affects us till our life's core

But if we believe in ourselves

As it's better to learn from those bits

Then I say go for it

As it's better to learn from those bits

Then only regret it later on

I will follow my heart

As it will lead me to my passion

And then using them together with my brain

I will follow my dream into reality

For it's what I wish for

And vow to accomplish

Irrespective of society's view

I always knew

Its what I want

And it's what I shall earn and not demand

I wish for it so I earn it

Neither bought it nor demanded it

For I had to prove to those

Who has always opposed
My dream for societies demand
For them, my dreams were nothing but fiction
As they couldn't do it
So how could I?
It's my chance to sho them
That I ain't a rag doll.

23. The New Me

The darkness within me is consuming me
Not unlike the sea
Hiding what we normally see
Maybe that's the key
As now I am able to do something which usually was forbidden
I crave to do something new
Which was imagined by only a few
I crave to make them proud
Those who said my head was in the cloud
This is all new for me too
Please take the clue
I want to follow my heart
And mark it as a new start
Can I please?
I really wish to taste the breeze
And have something I wish for now
No matter how
I will fulfill my dream
Even if the new me
And I finally feel free
In my own skin
And not like a bug on a pin.

24. Wondering Thoughts

Why do you think I did that?

Oh! I assure you I ain't a cat

Lovely day ahead of us

Are you taking the bus

I shall be walking towards my home

I have to read a book on something known as a gnome

May we get what we need

Go ahead and lead

For the sheep need a shepherd

Or they will be eaten by the leopard

Is it true

We are searching for something new

I wanna know

Will it have snow

They are just special

Even if they can constrict our blood vessel

I wonder how I will react

Will my mind start coming up with theories abstract

Love your passion

Along with your fashion

You have a lot of compassion

Make sure your face does not turn ashen

And last I wonder
Will my life truly turn into a blunder?

25. It's My Life & I Will Do What I Wish For

I crave the taste of reality

When I am stuck in the virtual world

Just like I crave the taste of virtuality

When I am in the real world

I wish for an escape

When my nightmare starts taking a shape

I cry my eyes out

Or just sit there with a pout

I may or may not talk with others

As it counts among my druthers

I choose what I do

I take an old path or new

For it's my wish

To eat which-ever chosen dish

I do what I think is right

What to do when in a plight

This is my life I wish to lead

And it will be my wounded which will bleed

I choose how to tend to them

And it will also be my dress whose I hold the hem

I thank you for your suggestion
But it ain't the answer to my question
I asked about who gave you the right to interfere
It's my life and I hope it's clear.

26. I Wish For My Life To Be Fair

Just because I am sad

Doesn't mean I am bad

Just because my emotions are suppressed

Doesn't mean that I am depressed

I may be just protecting myself

My heart may be similar to a certain elf

I could simply be an introvert

And that's why my words are usually curt

Anyways, this is me

If you can't handle then the door's open for you to flee

I don't care what you say

But cross the line and I will make you pay

You may not realize it now

I will destroy you completely and you will be left wondering just how?

Touch those I care about

And you will be at the end of your road even before you can shout

I warn you just once

As there won't be a warning issued before it's too late about
months
I dictate how I live my life
And not those for whom my decision are just another strife
I thank you for your care
But I wish my life to be fair.

27. No

I am 'No'
Just one word made of just 2 alphabets
Just a simple word
Used by all
Be it in different languages
But in the heart
Just a simple word
Known by all
But how many follow me?
Is it so hard
That you forget that all I have is a simple meaning
While you converted and used it as many
But in the heart
I am a disagreement
A way to disagreement
A way to express
Don't ignore me
I know you need me
And I am always there for you
So please
I beg you
Never forget me.

28. Money

Hello, I am 'Money'
A medium of exchange
Not some cloth which is in of laundering
Not a god damn status pin
I am misunderstood
Majorly misunderstood
And that's why I ask
Learn from the past and
Not to repeat it
Again and again
Till you get bored of me
And then replace me
Please, I beg you here
To save me
I beg you to save me
So you can not only save yourself but others too
Please.

29. A Moment

A moment is all it takes
To turn the cream like sweet dream
Into a nightmare
Filled with dead hare
A moment is all it takes
For our lives to end
And our wills to bend
A moment is all it takes
For us to cry a miniature flood
When we see the free-flowing blood
A moment that we don't cherish
Can lead us to perish
For us to turn from caring to overbearing
It could be the moment you regret
A moment is all it takes
For us to make a change
And change we make
But are they the right one
Or the easy one
Think of what you do
As it only takes you a moment
Only a moment indead.

30. Refuge From Danger

I wish for refuge

From a danger huge

I am scared

Because I know I won't be spared

As the problem is massive

And while being created, we were all passive

Now it's showing some response

And we did nothing but chit-chat for the nonse

I am wondering what's gonna happen

When danger chomps us down like a terrapin

And it scares me

Thinking of the dangers glee

When it takes its own revenge

And we will have nothing to avenge

Because it's us who started this

And all we could do will be hiss

Along with yowling in pain

As our too late efforts will all be in vain

For it's already too late

And its long past the due date.

9 7 9 8 8 8 8 3 3 0 2 4 1